Live Your Life With Attitude

Karen A Porter

ISBN:978-0-9905565-0-3
ISBN-10:0990556506

DEDICATION

This book is dedicated to YOU and your magnificent self. Live the life you want, the life you deserve, the life you were born to live.

Live Your Life With Attitude

Why, What, Who and When?

Have you ever been told to be less than or different from who you really are? Of course you have, wrong question.

Are you ready to BE exactly who you are, without explanation or apology? This book can help. Nobody knows you but you and if you are ready to be authentic, step up and show the world, I am here to cheer-lead and to give you a space to start practicing.

I am a truth teller, a smart ass, a thorn in the side of many, a faithful confidant, loyal friend, a loving, creative, powerful woman, humanitarian, mama bear and total bitch. I am a spiritual rabble-rouser and grounded pragmatist.

This book grew out my pairing old photos with smart remarks. I have made hundreds of "Cards With Attitude" using discarded vintage photos. Many people loved them and others found them rude, crude and lewd. But, universally, card sales have plummeted. Personal mail is becoming rare.

So, I am re-purposing my art, putting it in a form

Live Your Life With Attitude

that can be shared, enjoyed and used. Feel free to tear up the book to create you own cards or notes or illustrate your own journals.

This is a play book and a work book. Use it for whatever you like. Keep it by the phone for messages, write your to-do lists in it or use it as an illustrated journal. There are 52 attitudes just in case you want to use it as a weekly journal or record book. Opposite each page with photo collage, attitude and thoughts, lies a blank page ready for you to fill. Enjoy!

WARNING: If you are delicate, sheltered, or easily offended, CLOSE THIS BOOK AND WALK AWAY.

WARNING: If you think one way is the only way, then good luck on that path and CLOSE THIS BOOK AND WALK AWAY.

BUT....If you are ready to be the ONE and ONLY YOU (even if it is only for a little while, from time to time) ....

Yay! Whoo Hoo! Here's to YOU!

Live Your Life With Attitude

ACNOWLEDGMENTS

Thank you, my friends for your support and my family for so much raw material. I would like to acknowledge Kim Rudy, my #1 fan, (in that Kathy Bates/Misery way). No one will ever replace you.
Thank you Andrea Hylen and Heal My Voice.
Thank you Kathleen Nelson Troyer.
Thank you Dotti Drumm for being you.
My deepest love and greatest thanks I give to my husband David and to my boys, the son who must not be named and the other one.
 I am who I am thanks to you.

Live Your Life With Attitude

YOUR Life With Attitude

This is an invitation to you, whatever your attitude, to live your life authentically. You came into this world for a reason different from every other person's reason for being. You have a unique perspective and skill set.

I hope you already have support on this journey to an authentic life. If you do not feel supported, know there are like-minded people in the world just waiting for you to live your purpose.

You have the power to change your life. If you are waiting to 'find' the answers outside yourself or if you waiting to be rescued, you are going to be waiting forever. YOU have the answers. You might have to shift some thinking or release old beliefs or habits or routines. Only you can make those decisions and changes for yourself. Start with what you have, where you are, because it is the perfect place for now.

Use this journal as a place to explore and to practice attitudes. Have fun. Make it yours.

Live Your Life With Attitude

Everything is better at the beach.

Life's A Beach

We can't always be at the beach, or in the south of France or sipping a mojito, but we can find a way to have the beach/France/mojito attitude any time. So what would it take? What is the 'beach' for you? There is no right answer and so many possibilities...

Live Your Life With Attitude

Live Your Life With Attitude

I am not a bitch. I am THE bitch.

Be YOU!

Whatever you are, CLAIM AND OWN IT
I am **THE** bitch, **THE** mother, **THE** friend.
I am **THE ONE AND ONLY ME**.
You are THE ONE AND ONLY YOU!

4

Live Your Life With Attitude

Live Your Life With Attitude

Don't make me bitch-slap you.

Bad Attitude

No doubt, there are times when you want to hurt someone and you can argue it is deserved but IF you decide to take action, take responsibility for it. Nobody MAKES you do anything. You choose your behavior. Always.

Live Your Life With Attitude

Live Your Life With Attitude

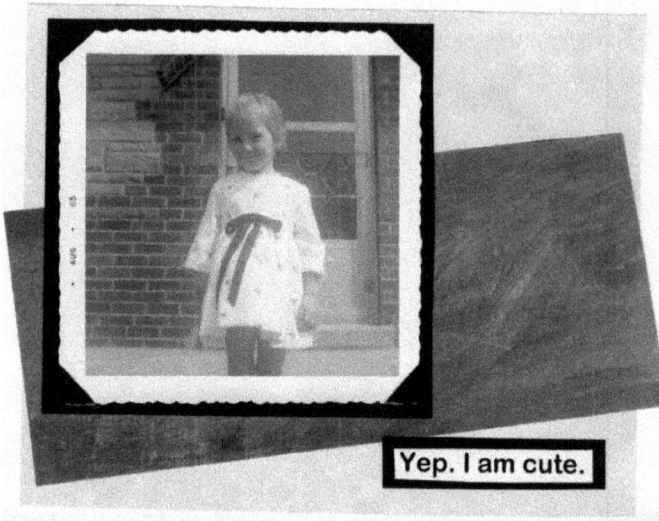

Yep. I am cute.

Work It Baby!

Everybody has a talent set, skills, and attributes. Recognize what works and WORK IT. You may find yourself walking the fine line between using your assets and being manipulative. Walk the line. Take a walk on the wild side and see what happens.

Live Your Life With Attitude

Live Your Life With Attitude

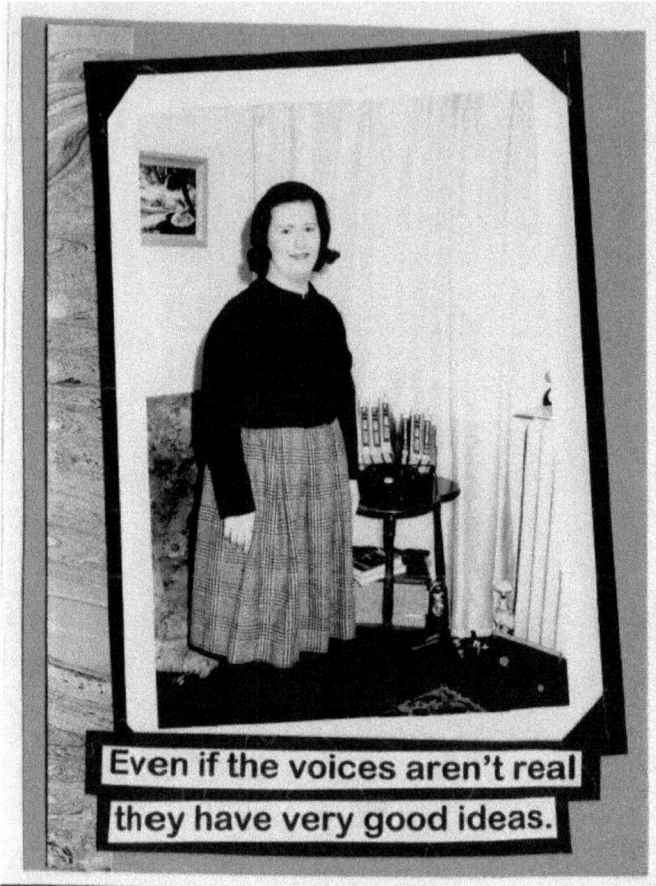

Even if the voices aren't real they have very good ideas.

Being Oblivious

Your happy place is good. Your fantasy life
is sweet and your imaginary friends are the best.
Don't let anyone tell you otherwise. Enjoy!

Live Your Life With Attitude

Live Your Life With Attitude

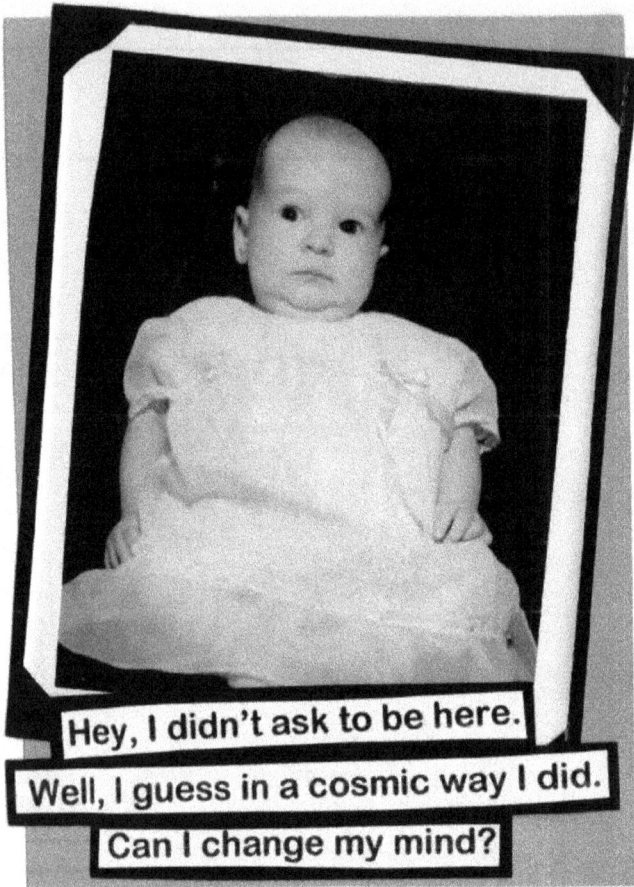

Hey, I didn't ask to be here.
Well, I guess in a cosmic way I did.
Can I change my mind?

Choose Your Attitude

Face it. You are here. You are you. Your family is your family. What happened is done. What you can choose is how you live today, relate to others and respond to situations. THAT is your only choice.

Live Your Life With Attitude

Live Your Life With Attitude

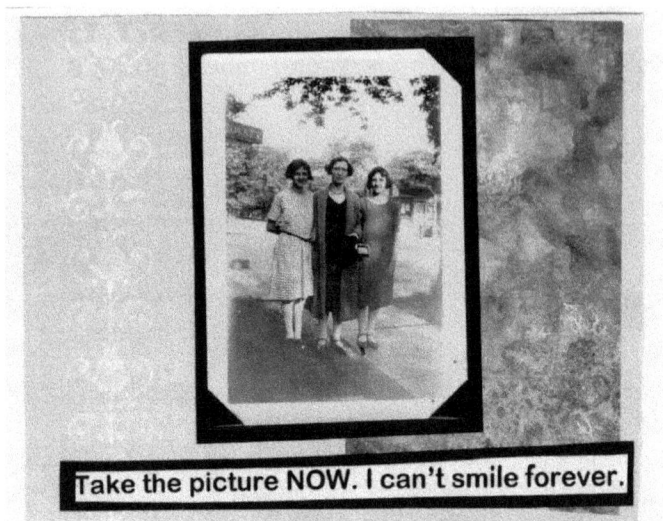

Take the picture NOW. I can't smile forever.

State Your Needs

Nobody can read you mind. Suffering in silence is stupid. Assuming that others will anticipate and fill your needs is grandiose fantasy. The world does not know what you need until you put it out there for all to hear. Then there is a chance of getting what you want. Maybe not a big chance, but at least it enters the realm of possibility.

Live Your Life With Attitude

Live Your Life With Attitude

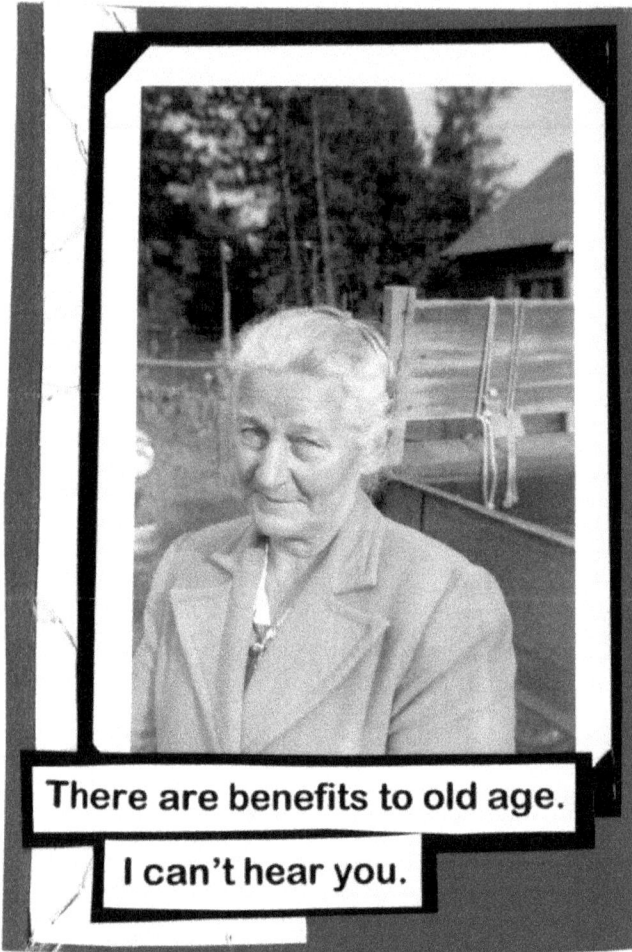

There are benefits to old age.

I can't hear you.

Acceptance

What if there is an up side to everything?
Hearing going? You can ignore annoying people.
Sight not great? You won't see new chin hairs!

Live Your Life With Attitude

Live Your Life With Attitude

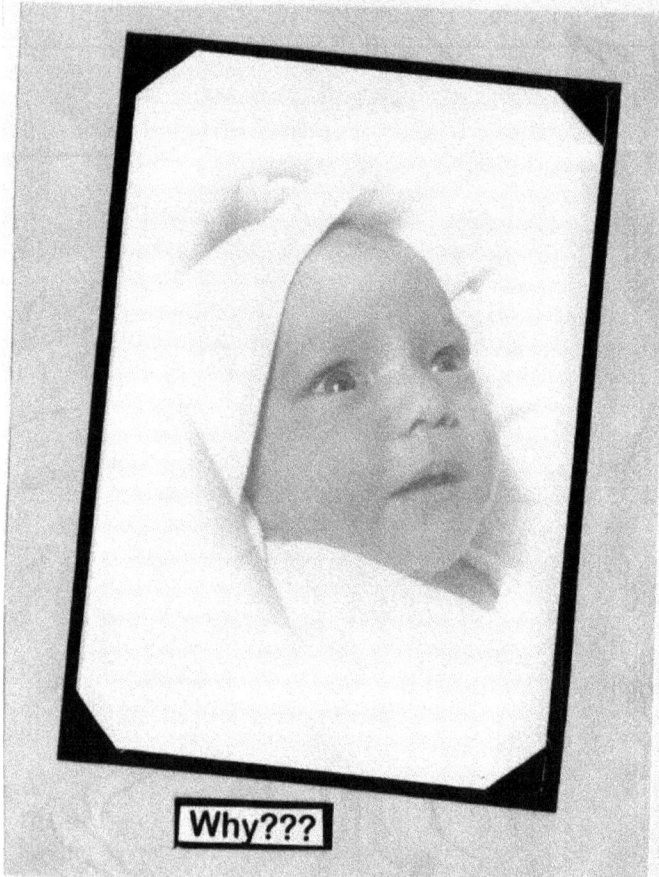

Why???

Acceptance

Shit happens. Sometimes we recognize the lesson, other times the why of it is beyond reason. At those times, can you find the faith to trust that in some way, it makes sense and it is exactly what had to happen for you to get to the next step along the path?

18

Live Your Life With Attitude

Live Your Life With Attitude

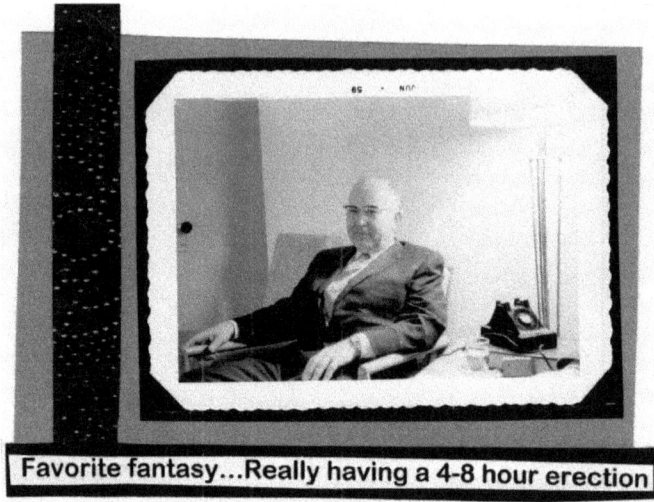

Favorite fantasy...Really having a 4-8 hour erection

Dream Big, Baby

Your dreams are yours. Every other person on the face of the earth may call them stupid, impossible, or ridiculous. If it is your dream, hold it close and watch it grow (probably not the best choice of words for this photo...) I don't want your dreams. I may not even want to know about your dreams. I have my own, thank you very much.

Live Your Life With Attitude

Live Your Life With Attitude

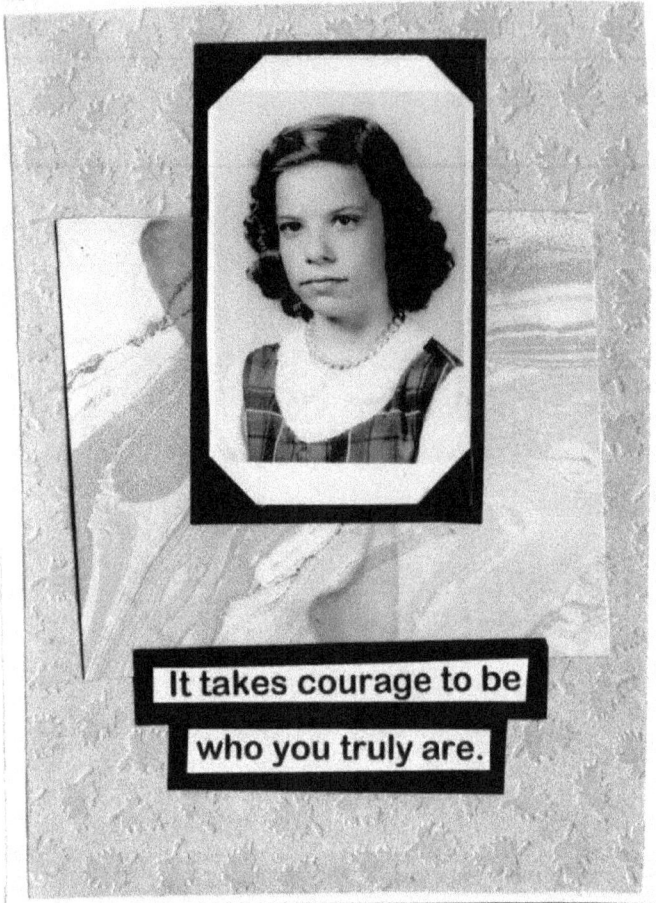

It takes courage to be
who you truly are.

Authenticity

Fear keeps us from being who we really are. We can stay in fear, live small and safe by pretending to be who we think we should be or who others want us to be or we can grow a pair and live an authentic life.

Live Your Life With Attitude

Live Your Life With Attitude

Favorite fantasy...Altar Boys

Keeping It In Check

Know the difference between having thoughts and taking action. Also know the risk you take in sharing all those socially unacceptable, immoral and potentially illegal if acted upon fantasies with others.

Live Your Life With Attitude

Live Your Life With Attitude

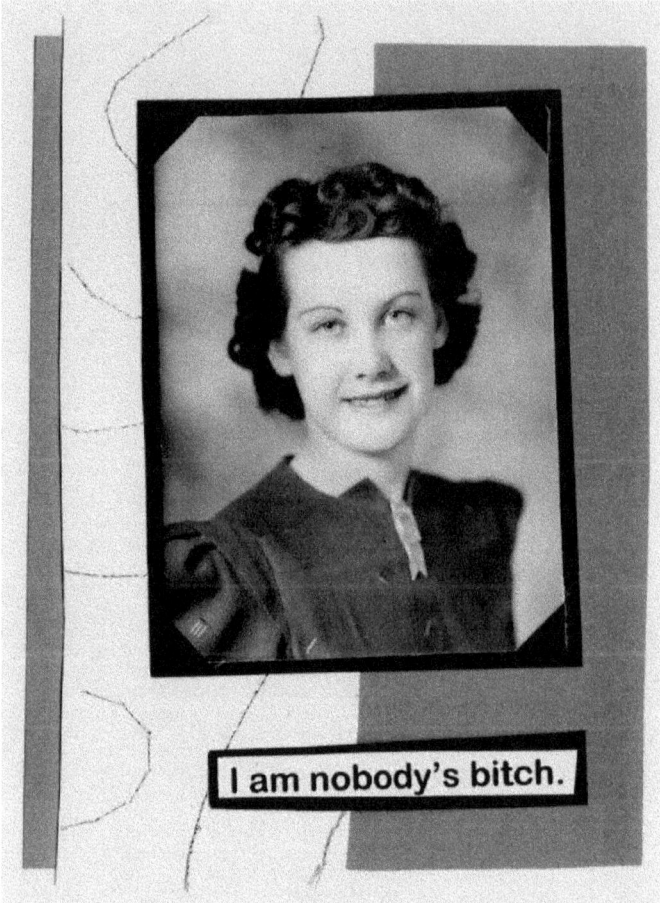

I am nobody's bitch.

Autonomy

Be here for YOU and you will be here for everyone else. Being your best self lets you be the best parent, spouse or friend. Being a doormat serves no one, hurts too many and robs the world of YOU.

Live Your Life With Attitude

Live Your Life With Attitude

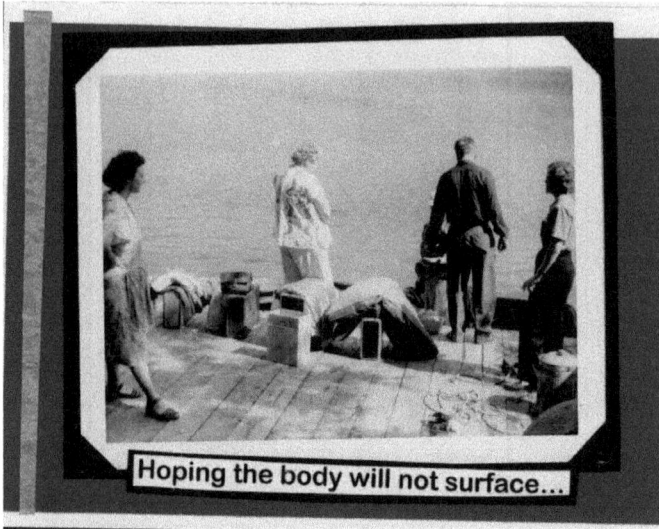

Hoping the body will not surface...

Be Subtle and Self Assured

Some may say 'smart and sneaky.' No matter what you call it, you can do just about anything if you have the right attitude. Never sign in at a front desk again. The energy you project determines how you are treated. You know exactly what I'm talkin' 'bout. You know people who do this very successfully. Now it's your turn.

Live Your Life With Attitude

Live Your Life With Attitude

Favorite fantasy... Granny's Brazier

Surprise! Surprise! Surprise!

You will never truly know anyone but yourself. Even that can be the adventure of a lifetime. We all have many facets, much depth and unlimited potential. Enjoy the exploration!

Live Your Life With Attitude

Live Your Life With Attitude

Bon Voyage!

Anticipation

Vacations can be fabulous, amazing, and rejuvenating. They can also be stress-filled, over planned and exhausting. Sometimes the anticipation of a getaway is enough to get you through a rough patch. Maybe the trick is to always have something you are happily awaiting. Having a coffee exactly the way you love it, taking a cool shower during a hot day or using the lemon verbena soap you have been saving can feel delightfully luxurious. Stop SAVING and begin SAVORING. Think of how many things you could look forward to and how many ways you can treat yourself to that restorative feeling of a getaway.

Live Your Life With Attitude

Live Your Life With Attitude

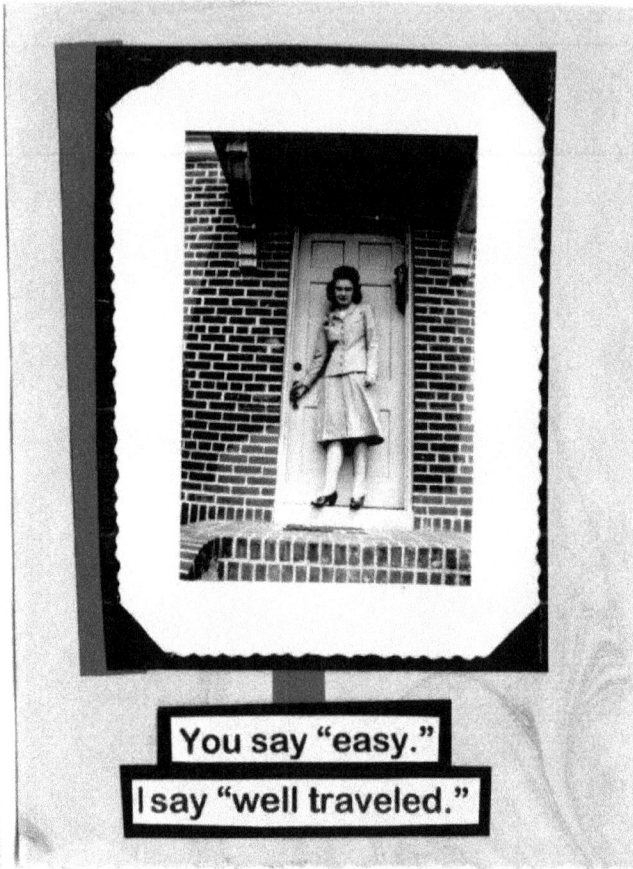

You say "easy."
I say "well traveled."

It's <u>Your</u> Problem, Hon

When one is maligned or labeled, it says more about the one passing judgment than the one being judged. Know what is yours to own and what does not belong to you. If it's not yours, stay strong and do not take it on. Let it pass you by and keep going.

Live Your Life With Attitude

Live Your Life With Attitude

Do you think I am amused?

Tell It Like It Is

Tell it like it is. Speak your truth. Let it loose. Screw pretending, being nice all the time or keeping the peace at any price. Keeping it real allows you to ride the peaks and valleys of each day and deal with what comes up in the moment. Would you rather address something in a timely manner or hang onto a resentment for years? Deal with it and be done. Sometimes dealing with it will mean breaking ties or walking away. You get to decide.

Live Your Life With Attitude

Live Your Life With Attitude

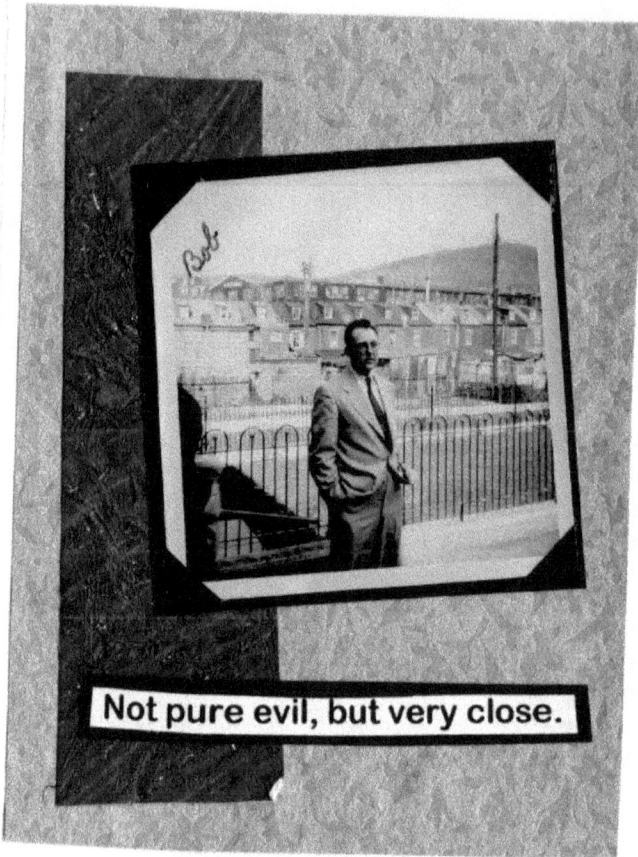

Not pure evil, but very close.

You Have The Power

Face it. People do awful things, some are pros at it. You get to choose who you want in your life. Just because you are related or have until now filled a certain role, you do not have to continue. It is your life, your choice. Only YOU can change how and with whom you live. Bastards be gone!

Live Your Life With Attitude

Live Your Life With Attitude

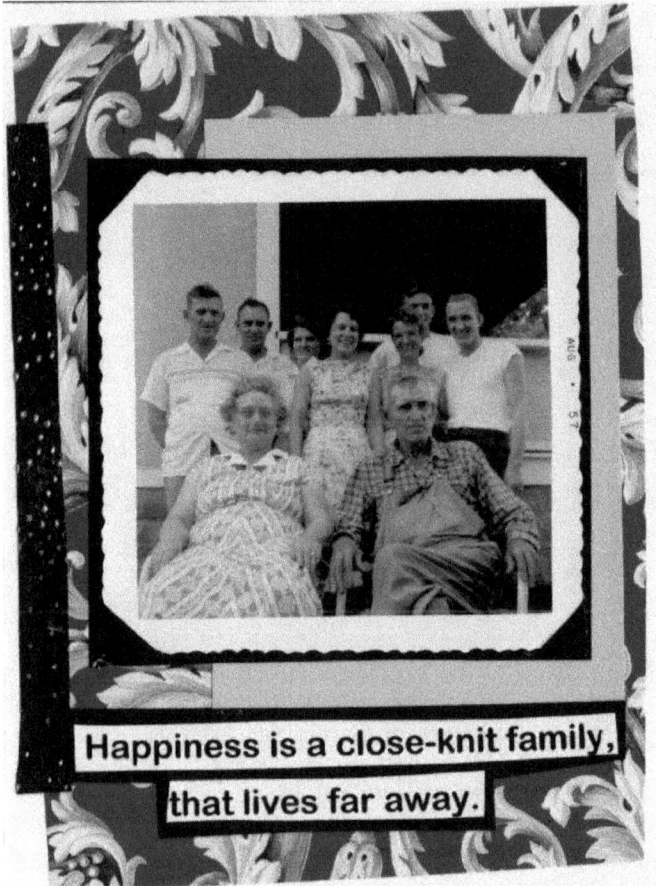

Happiness is a close-knit family, that lives far away.

Can't Live With Them......

Family is a fact. You can choose if and how you continue to relate to them. People come into and leave our lives. Nothing is forever even though it can feel like forever. All relationships end. You can choose the terms.

Live Your Life With Attitude

Live Your Life With Attitude

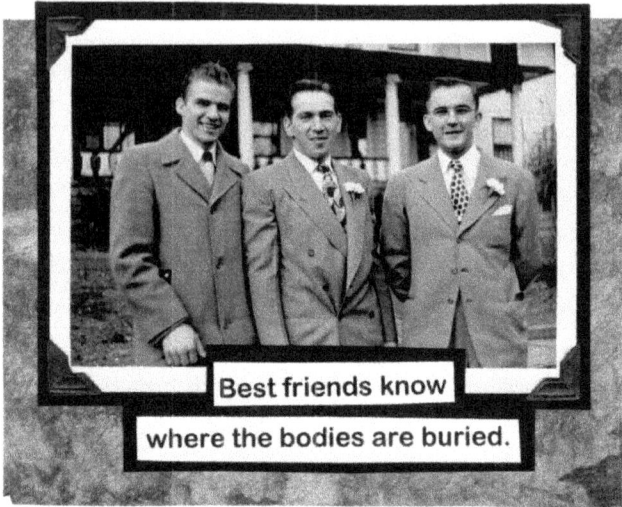

Best friends know where the bodies are buried.

Choose Your Friends Wisely

Trust is earned and can be easily broken. Good friends are precious and few. Treat them well and hope you will be treated in kind. A true friend will take your secrets to the grave even if you don't have the same amount of dirt on them.

Live Your Life With Attitude

Live Your Life With Attitude

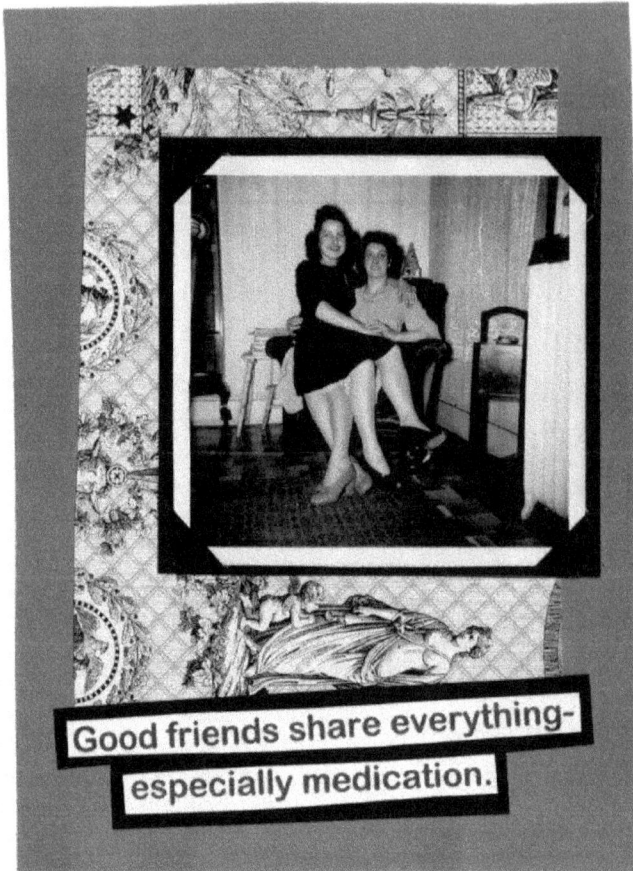

Good friends share everything—especially medication.

Be Generous

It costs you nothing to be kind. Be as generous as you can with your time and talents. You have no idea how you impact someone with a compliment or pleasant observation. It usually goes unseen, but there is always a ripple effect. You choose the tone.

Live Your Life With Attitude

Live Your Life With Attitude

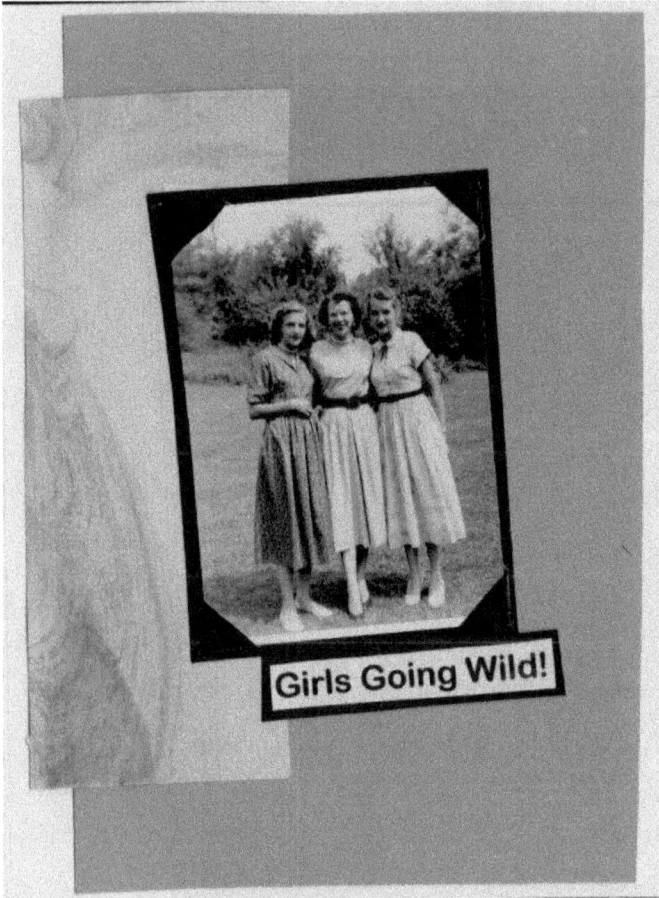

Girls Going Wild!

Does Fun Hunt You Down?

Do you let yourself have fun? Could you allow more fun into your day to day? Can you imagine enjoying your life so much that it seems that fun finds you no matter when it is or where you are? Remember, there is no such thing as too much fun.

Live Your Life With Attitude

Live Your Life With Attitude

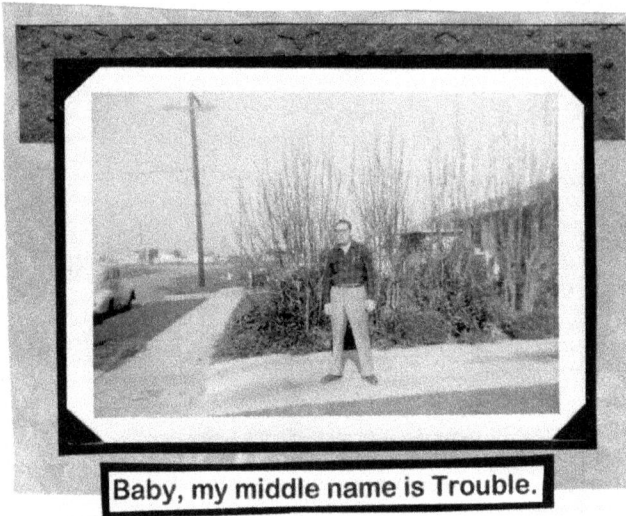

Baby, my middle name is Trouble.

Sometimes Delusional Is Great

Whatever you say, hon. If it makes you happy, go for it. Wear a superhero costume under your suit. Be James Bond in your spare time. Declare yourself the Queen of Crazyville. We all self delude to some degree. No harm, no foul as long as it all stays in your happy place.

Live Your Life With Attitude

Live Your Life With Attitude

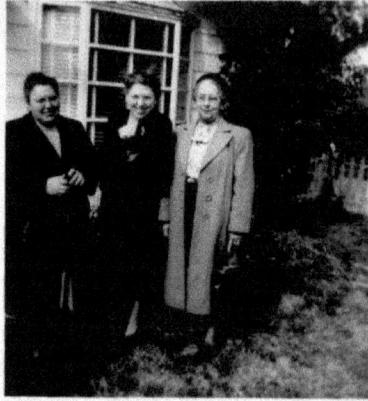

Hon, if being awesome was a crime,
We'd be a serving life.

Know Your Worth

Damn, you rock it. Don't listen to anybody who wants you to dim your light. The world needs you to be all you, all the time. It's a 24/7 job and only you can do it. Whoo Hoo!

Live Your Life With Attitude

Live Your Life With Attitude

Life is good.

Satisfaction

Being happy with who you are and what you have is the greatest gift you can give yourself. If you can enjoy what is, you will enjoy all that will be. If you believe that you need anything to be different in order to be happy, sorry hon, it will never be enough.

Live Your Life With Attitude

Live Your Life With Attitude

Red Hot Mama

Embodiment

Whatever it is that you are, feel it fully, on a cellular level, magnify it with each breath and manifest it in every action. Be you. It is your prime directive and most important work.

Live Your Life With Attitude

Live Your Life With Attitude

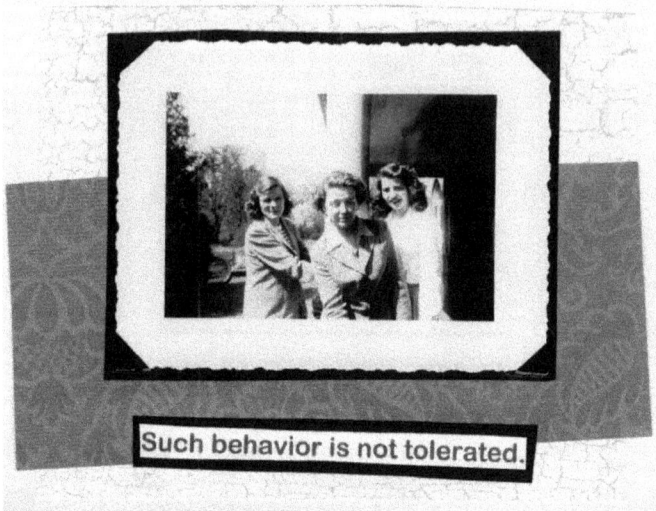

Such behavior is not tolerated.

Boundaries and Flexibility

Set limits, have rules, make them known and be ready to change. You can be firm and flexible, an enforcer and forgiving. Having and maintaining standards is not the same as having a pole up your ass. If however, there comes a time when you discover the presence of a pole-like item in the aforementioned orifice, you can always choose to remove it. It is not the most graceful of processes but you will survive. I have, repeatedly.

Live Your Life With Attitude

Live Your Life With Attitude

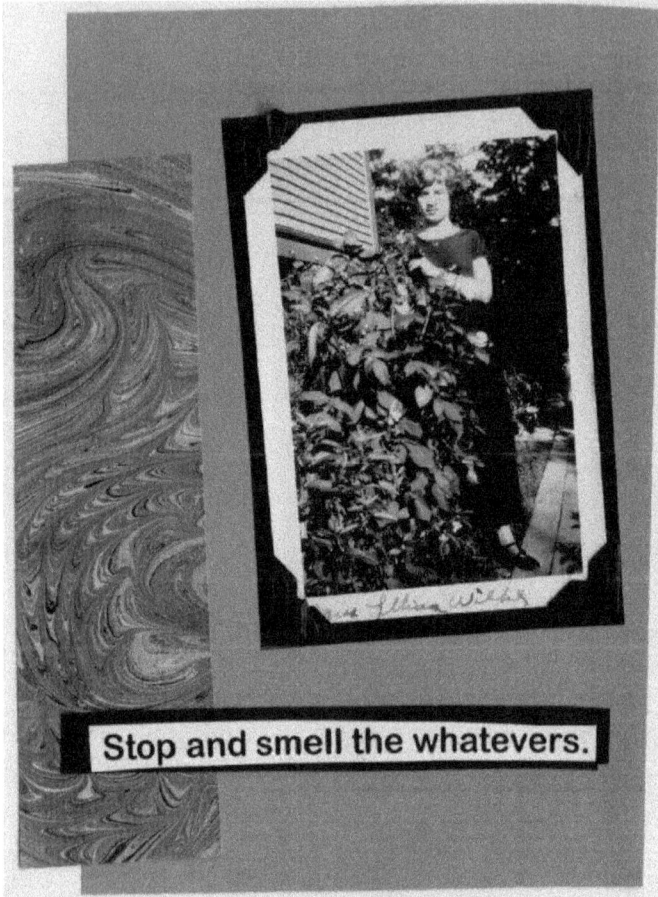

Stop and smell the whatevers.

Appreciation

Life is full of wonder and beauty. Taking time to experience what is present in the moment makes life juicy. Small details, noticed and gathered create a full and varied collection, forming a very rich life.

Live Your Life With Attitude

Live Your Life With Attitude

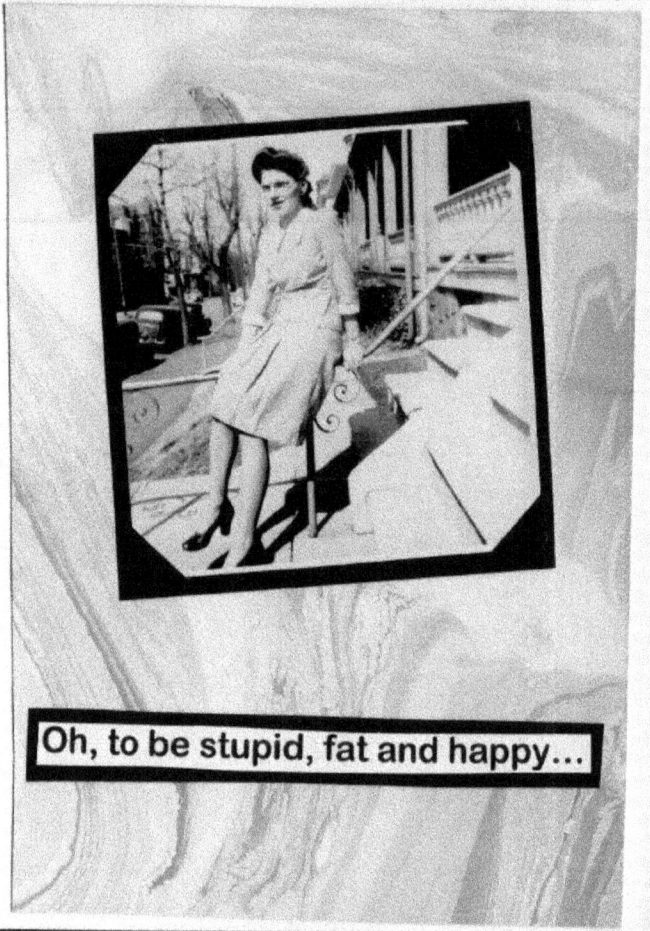

Oh, to be stupid, fat and happy...

Awake and Aware

Life gets more challenging after you wake up to your purpose. Doing the work does not make life less complicated or without struggle. Staying asleep seems easier but is that what you really want?

Live Your Life With Attitude

Live Your Life With Attitude

Obey the rules, miss the fun.

Being a Selective Scofflaw

There are rules worth following but some are just stupid. It is true that some rules are meant to be broken, others bent or totally ignored. Sometimes being a little bad is a very good thing. How bad are you? How bad do you want to be? How much bad is just right?

Live Your Life With Attitude

Live Your Life With Attitude

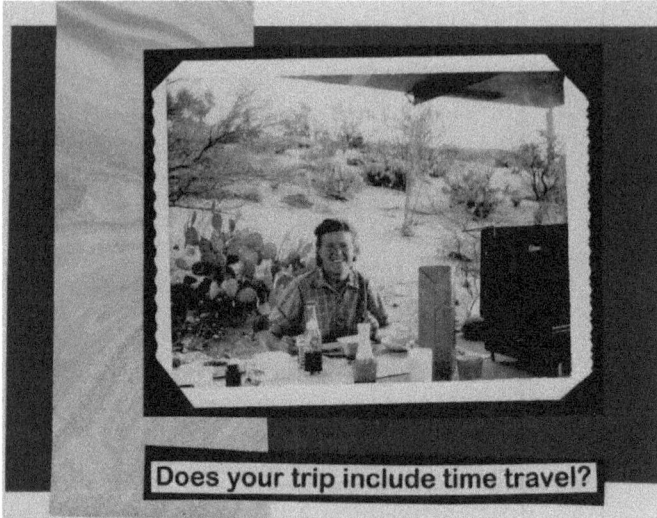

Does your trip include time travel?

Make it Right

So what if time travel is still theoretical? There are re-do's and do-overs. You can always make amends, be honest about your feelings and take responsibility for your past actions. At my 40th high school reunion, imagine my surprise when a class bully, confronted with the effects of his actions, apologized and owned being an asshole back then. Sometimes, life is very sweet.

Live Your Life With Attitude

Live Your Life With Attitude

I am not a real bitch.

I just play one in your life.

Choose Your Roles

We all have roles in life- child, parent, partner, spouse or friend. Some roles we take on, others are assigned. You get to choose which ones you fill and how you play each role.

Live Your Life With Attitude

Live Your Life With Attitude

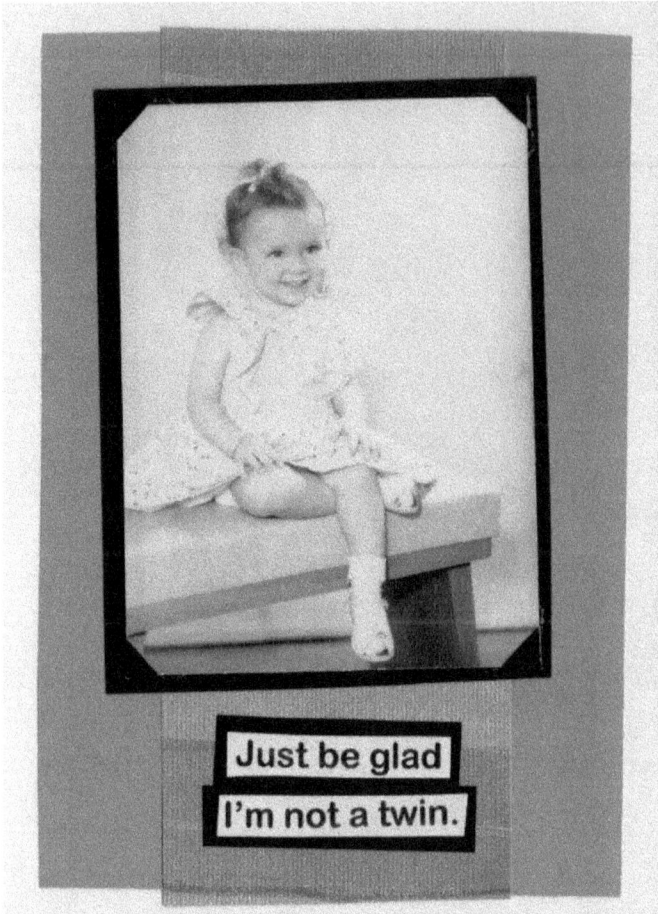

Just be glad
I'm not a twin.

Attitude of Gratitude

No matter what is driving you nuts, it could always be worse. No matter what the situation or relationship, there is something about it that is good or has value. Practice gratitude, goddammit.

Live Your Life With Attitude

Live Your Life With Attitude

Watch the hands, buddy.

Discretion

Embarrassing shit happens. We all make mistakes and do stupid stuff. Unfortunately, sometimes those things are recorded for the entire world to see repeatedly and forever. Discretion can keep a minor stupidity from becoming fodder for cable comedy routines.

Live Your Life With Attitude

Live Your Life With Attitude

You'll just wish you were dead.

Be Careful What You Wish For

There are things we want because we think we should want them or we are told it would be best. Be honest. Do you want it, really want it or are you following the path most traveled? One man's meat is another man's poison. What is perfect for me could drive you to an asylum or long to be in a coma. The illusion that the unchosen other is better is just that- an illusion.

Live Your Life With Attitude

Live Your Life With Attitude

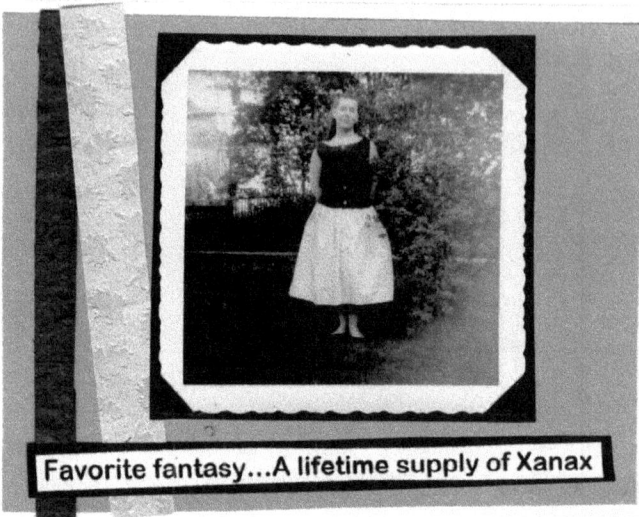

Favorite fantasy...A lifetime supply of Xanax

Coping or Crutch? You Decide

What is it that you do to get by or cope with challenges or stress? Is it helping or hurting? Compulsive eating or shopping is distracting for the moment but there is a price. Depending on medication or drinking can numb feeling but the underlying issues remain. We do the best we can until we can do differently or better. Once we have options, we can choose how to cope and take responsibility for those decisions.

Live Your Life With Attitude

Live Your Life With Attitude

I told you I was trouble.

Believe

People usually won't tell you but believe what their actions say. You are the only person you can change.

Live Your Life With Attitude

Live Your Life With Attitude

Kinky as a cheap garden hose.

MYOB

Your kinky could be my normal. Who cares? Live your life, without harming yourself or others. To each their own. Bless your sweet heart.

Live Your Life With Attitude

Live Your Life With Attitude

Grannies Gone Wild.

Everybody Has Their Moments

My great grandmother kept a pistol under her carriage blanket when going to market. A great-aunt was a wild flapper girl. A grandfather by marriage lost an eye, supposedly because a mule kicked him, but actually because his still exploded. Our mothers and grandmothers took on male roles and work during the war. Our ancestors, suffragists, pioneers, slaves and slave owners, camp survivors, business owners, hippies, feminists, soldiers and pacifists, were strong and wild men and women. Because they were, we are.

Live Your Life With Attitude

Live Your Life With Attitude

I am still hot. Only now, I am hot in flashes.

Adapting, Adjusting

Every day brings change. Being able to adapt to the changes life brings makes it easier. Bette Davis said that growing old is not for sissies. Amen Sister Bette. Courage to us all.

Live Your Life With Attitude

Live Your Life With Attitude

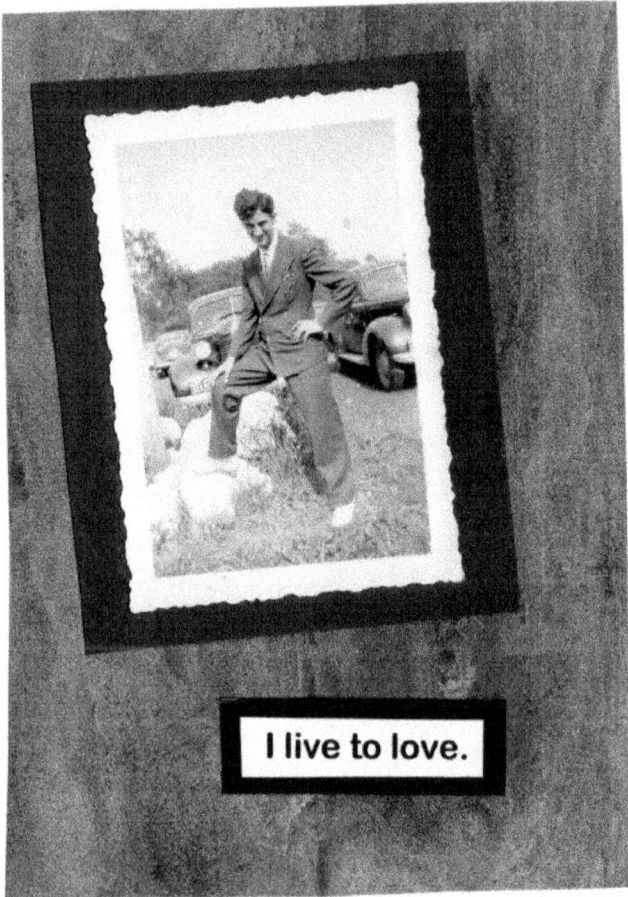

I live to love.

Passion

It doesn't matter whether you live to love, sing, garden, write, build, create, teach, make kitten videos or do the New York Times crossword puzzle in ink. Whatever your passion is, do it!

Live Your Life With Attitude

Live Your Life With Attitude

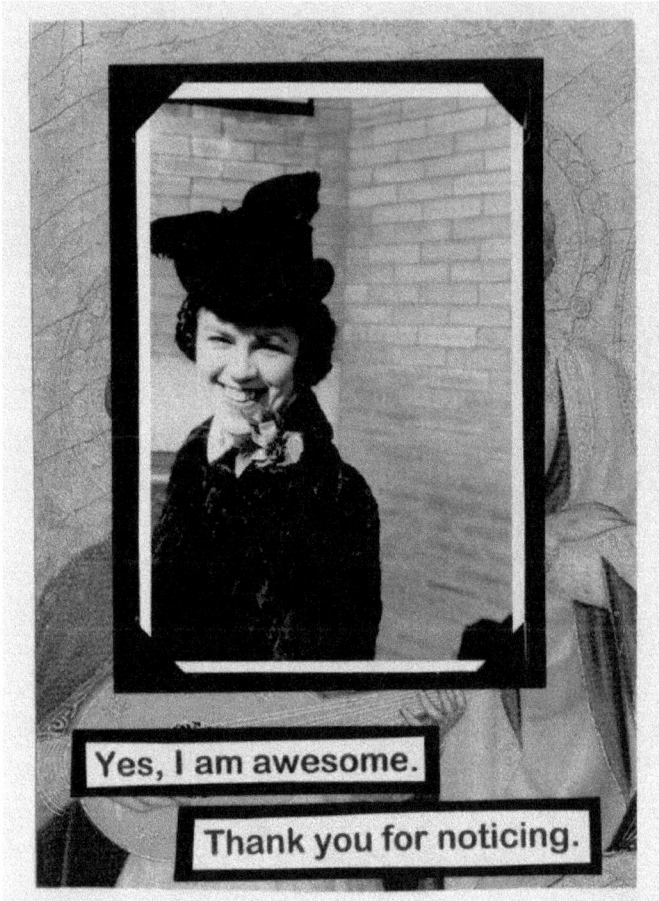

Yes, I am awesome.

Thank you for noticing.

Receiving

"Thank you" is the appropriate response to a compliment. Compliments are gifts. Tolerate the discomfort and open to receive. You are deserving. Repeat after me, "Thank you."

Live Your Life With Attitude

Live Your Life With Attitude

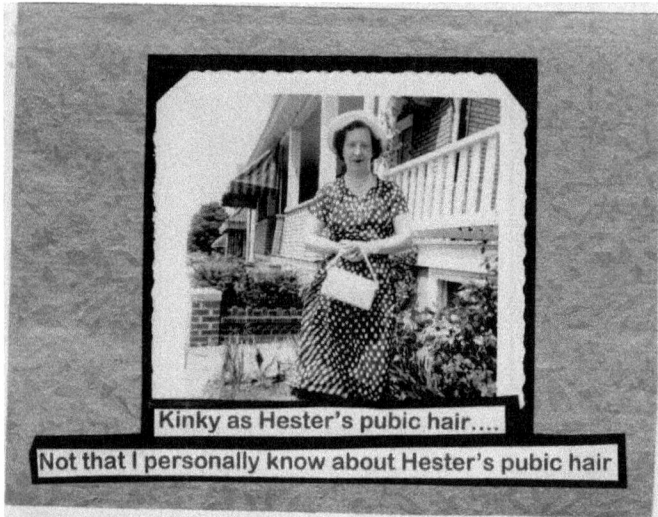

Kinky as Hester's pubic hair....

Not that I personally know about Hester's pubic hair

Plausible Deniability

I really don't need to know. Don't tell me. I don't want to know. Why do you have the need to share? In one generation we have gone from discretion to life in a fishbowl. I don't know that we can ever go back to the innocence of not knowing about our leaders' sexual behaviors but really, why do we care? You can tune out as much as you want. Turn off the talking heads, ignore the tabloids at the grocery store. My life is interesting enough and if I want drama, I know who to call.

Live Your Life With Attitude

Live Your Life With Attitude

Party girl.

You Are Who You Are

We come into this world who we are and we become more of who we are as we grow and experience life. Were you a social, happy baby or a screaming crabby-pants? The two year old's problems foretell the 12 and 22 year old's issues. Fortunately, predisposition does not set the future. It may color it but remember, you do have the power. You may have been born a party girl but you get to choose what parties you attend and how hard you party.

Live Your Life With Attitude

Live Your Life With Attitude

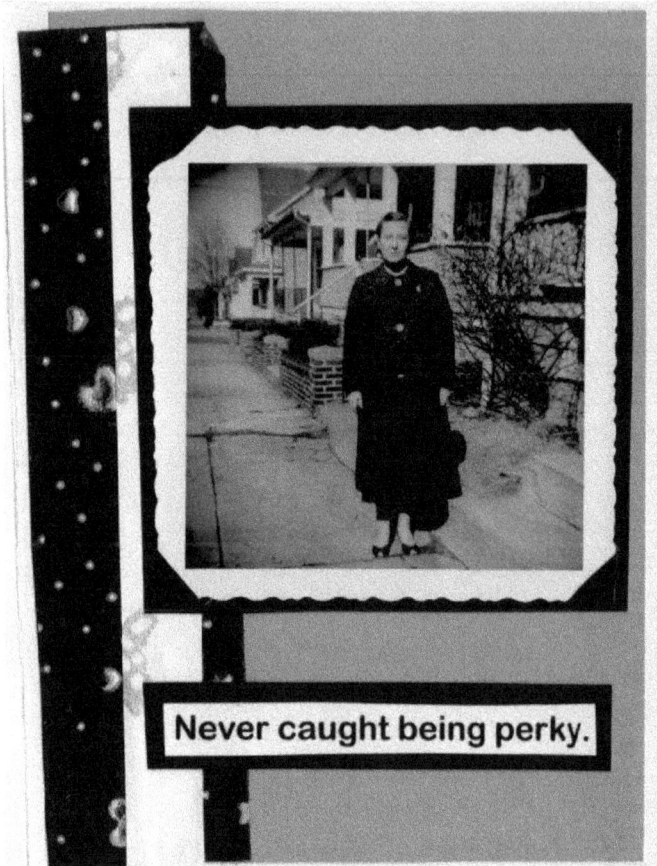

Never caught being perky.

Be Consistent

There is nothing wrong with shaking things up now and then but consistency has its charm. Dependability does not have to equal predictability but dependability can foster security and trust.

Live Your Life With Attitude

Live Your Life With Attitude

I am smiling.
That alone should scare you.

Trust Your Gut

Follow your instincts. How many times have you regretted not listening to that inner voice? Your intuition is the most powerful tool in your spiritual toolbox. Learn to trust it.

Live Your Life With Attitude

Live Your Life With Attitude

I think you're swell.

How Are YOU Hiding?

Step out of the shadows of fear. By living openly and fully who you are, you will find your true friends, deepest love and create the life you came here to live. That benefits everyone.

Live Your Life With Attitude

Live Your Life With Attitude

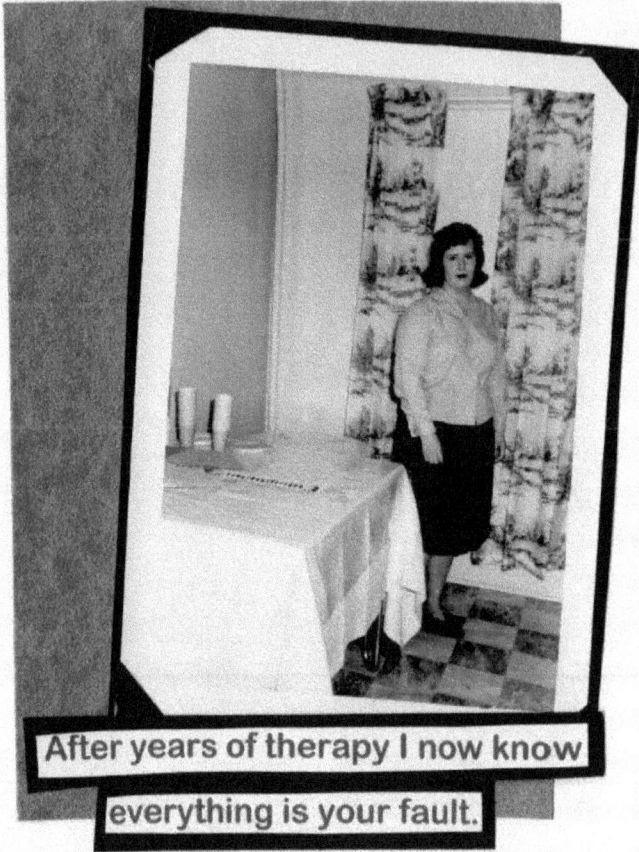

After years of therapy I now know everything is your fault.

Take Responsibility

The blame game is great until you realize that it gives all your power to someone else. You did not ask to be hurt or abused but you have total control over how you react, respond and continue living. Taking responsibility is reclaiming power.

Live Your Life With Attitude

Live Your Life With Attitude

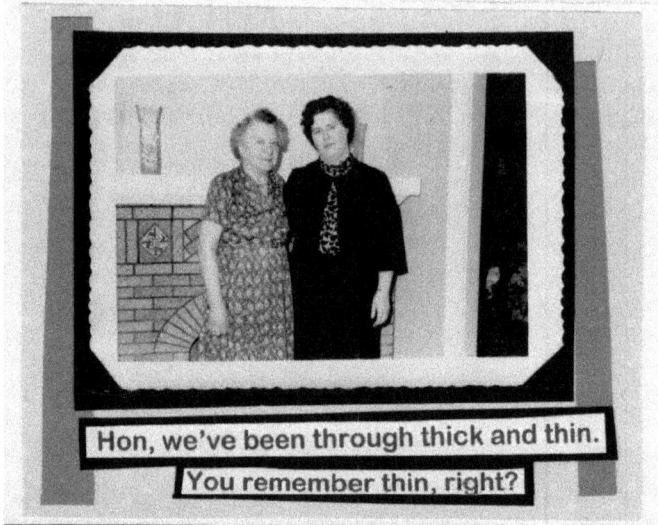

Hon, we've been through thick and thin. You remember thin, right?

Love Them Anyway

Don't you hate back-handed compliments? People say stupid shit. Some of us speak before self-censoring. You have a choice. You can smack them, return the insult, make a joke, or accept them for who they are no matter what craziness they spew. Pick your battles. Some things need to be addressed, others can be easily released. And when needed, you can love them from a distance.

Live Your Life With Attitude

Live Your Life With Attitude

Please tell me I'm adopted.

Individuality

Oh hon, it's rough for all of us. Feeling different, misunderstood and unappreciated is universal. Once you realize that the only acceptance you need is your own, when you fully love and appreciate yourself, you will need nothing more. Promise.

Live Your Life With Attitude

Live Your Life With Attitude

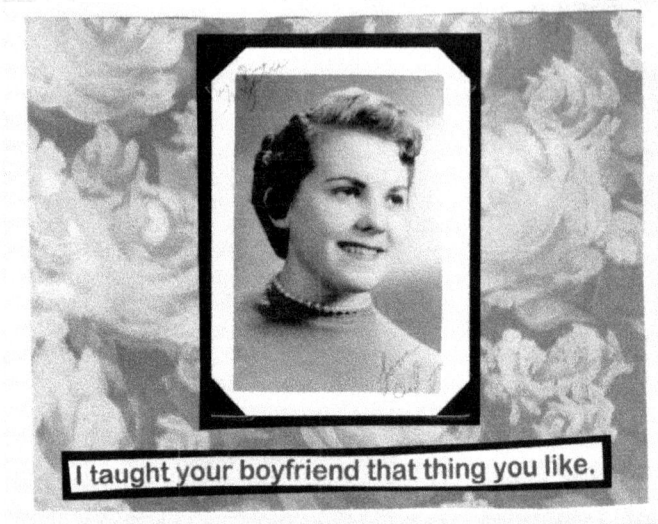

I taught your boyfriend that thing you like.

MAKING PEACE WITH THE PAST

Everybody has one. Usually the past is a mix of funny, painful, tragic, mildly embarrassing and totally humiliating. The one thing everyone's past has in common is that it is done. Over. Game, set, match. You can replay it, live there, wallow in it, bemoan and play victim. You can also deny, ignore and repeat. I choose to acknowledge, reflect, learn what I can, accept and go on. Peace with the past gives you calm in the present, unless you are fixated on the future, focused on what everyone else thinks about you and terrified to make a decision. Your life, your choice. Always.

Live Your Life With Attitude

Live Your Life With Attitude

Live Your Life With Attitude

ABOUT THE AUTHOR

Karen Porter was born a Balmer Hon and continues to live in Baltimore, MD with her husband, David, two sons and three cats. A writer, artist, teacher and humanitarian, Karen loves being a support and cheerleader for others to be all they want to be.

Contact Karen at Karen@mamaporter.com or visit her website www.mamaporter.com

ABOUT THE COVER

That happy, sassy little girl is the author. The photo was taken a few months before eight years of progressively violent sexual abuse began. I, Karen Porter, own all that I was and am. Attitude absolutely got me into lots of hot water, got me out of trouble, helped me survive extensive abuse, heal and thrive.

Live Your Life With Attitude